UNDERSTAND YOUR

Mind AND Body

Anxiety

Adelaide Wilder

e Explore other books at:
WWW.ENGAGEBOOKS.COM

VANCOUVER, B.C.

e→ WWW.ENGAGEBOOKS.COM

Anxiety: Understand Your Mind and Body
Wilder, Adelaide 1994 –
Text © 2023 Engage Books
Design © 2023 Engage Books

Edited by: A.R. Roumanis Ashley Lee,
Melody Sun, and Sarah Harvey
Design by: Mandy Christiansen

Text set in Montserrat Regular.
Chapter headings set in Hobgoblin.

This book is not meant to replace the advice of a medical professional or be a tool for diagnosis. It is an educational tool to help children understand what they or other people are going through.

FIRST EDITION / FIRST PRINTING

Photo of Selena Gomez by Mikey Hennessy. Photo of Elliot Page by Elliot Page. Photo of Chris Evans by Gage Skidmore. Every reasonable effort has been made to contact the copyright holders of all material reproduced in this book.

LIBRARY AND ARCHIVES CANADA CATALOGUING IN PUBLICATION

Title: Anxiety / Adelaide Wilder.
Names: Wilder, Adelaide, 1994- author.
Description: Series statement: Understand your mind and body

Identifiers: Canadiana (print) 20230219896 | Canadiana (ebook) 2023021990X
ISBN 978-1-77476-772-6 (hardcover)
ISBN 978-1-77476-773-3 (softcover)
ISBN 978-1-77476-774-0 (epub)
ISBN 978-1-77476-775-7 (pdf)
ISBN 978-1-77878-106-3 (audio)

Subjects:
LCSH: Anxiety in children—Juvenile literature.
LCSH: Anxiety—Treatment—Juvenile literature.
LCSH: Anxiety—Juvenile literature.

Classification: LCC BF723.A5 W55 2023 | DDC J155.4/1246—DC23

This project has been made possible in part by the Government of Canada.

Canada 🍁

Contents

4   What Is Anxiety?

6   What Causes Anxiety?

8   How Does Anxiety Affect Your Brain?

10 How Does Anxiety Affect Your Body?

12 Kinds of Anxiety

14 Does Anxiety Go Away?

16 Asking for Help

18 How to Help Others With Anxiety

20 The History of Anxiety

22 Anxiety Superheroes

24 Anxiety Tip 1: Mindfulness

26 Anxiety Tip 2:
    Noticing Triggers

28 Anxiety Tip 3: Spotting
    False Thoughts

30 Quiz

What Is Anxiety?

Anxiety is an intense feeling of worry, fear, or panic that is hard to control. **Stress** can cause people to have anxiety. Everyone feels a small amount of anxiety sometimes.

KEY WORD

Stress: when people feel uncomfortable about something that is happening.

Some people deal with anxiety all the time. When that happens, it might become an anxiety disorder. An anxiety disorder is a **mental illness** where you feel extreme or constant worry.

KEY WORD

Mental illness: an illness that affects how you think, feel, and behave.

What Causes Anxiety?

Genetics are traits that are passed down from one family member to another. They are one reason some people have anxiety. If Someone's family has anxiety, they are more likely to have it as well.

Many events or experiences can also cause anxiety.

- Stress over work or school
- Fights with friends or family
- Worries about money
- Problems with mental or physical health
- **Trauma**
- Side effects from medicine
- Illness

KEY WORD

Trauma: a physical or emotional reaction to harmful experiences. The effects of trauma can stay with people for a long time.

How Does Anxiety Affect Your Brain?

Anxiety affects three parts of the brain: the **brain stem**, the **limbic system**, and the **frontal lobe**. The brain stem keeps a person's body alive. The limbic system manages how one feels. The frontal lobe helps the thinking process.

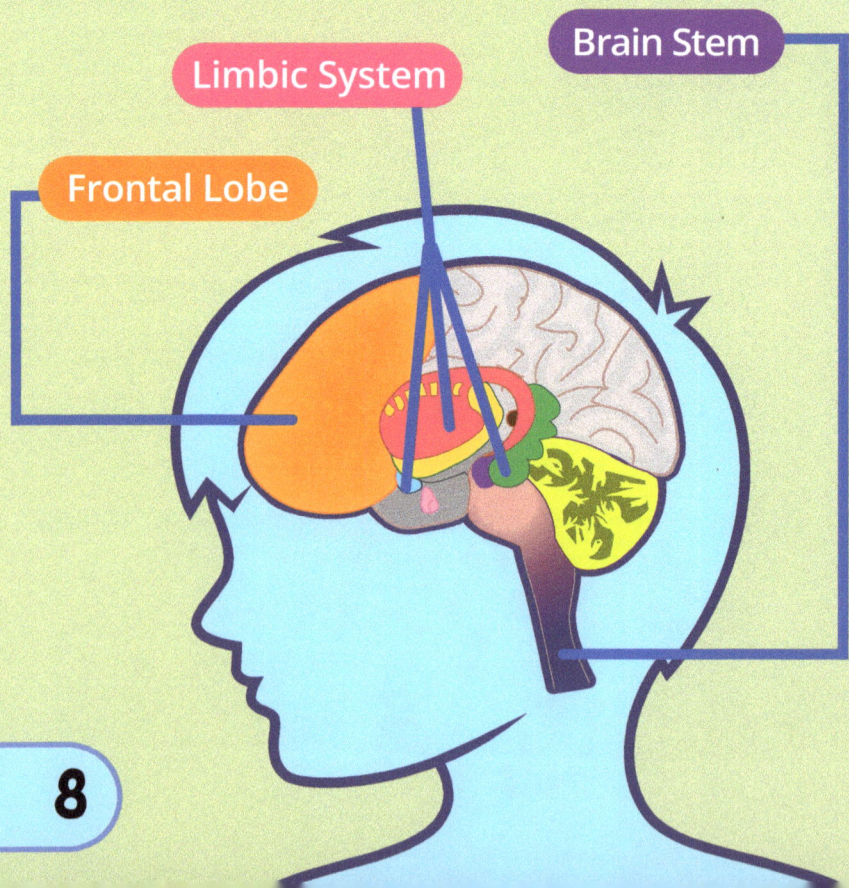

Brain Stem

Limbic System

Frontal Lobe

When someone is anxious, they might feel confused, angry, or tired all the time. They might be filled with fear or worry. That makes it hard to think clearly. Learning new things might take longer.

How Does Anxiety Affect Your Body?

When someone feels anxious, their brain orders their body to react. They may feel their hands getting clammy, their heart racing, or butterflies in their stomach. This is called a stress response. Stress responses are meant to keep people safe in dangerous situations.

The stress response is sometimes called the fight, flight, or freeze response.

People might get lightheaded or feel sick to their stomach when they feel very anxious. Their heart rate might increase. They might feel more alert. Some people might even have a **panic attack**.

KEY WORD

Panic attack: a sudden moment of intense anxiety. It happens when the body thinks it is in danger even when it is not.

Kinds of Anxiety Disorders

Anxiety disorders show up in different ways. Some people feel extreme fear when they see a certain object or when they experience certain things. This is called a phobia.

Social anxiety disorder is a kind of phobia. It makes you anxious about being around other people.

Some people feel very anxious about everyday events and activities. This is called generalized anxiety disorder. It may happen to people with **depression**.

KEY WORD

Depression: a mental illness that causes strong feelings of sadness and lack of hope.

Around 10 percent of children experience an anxiety disorder.

Does Anxiety Go Away?

A small amount of anxiety will come and go during everyone's life. Anxiety disorders are more difficult to manage. If anxiety disorders are not treated, they may become worse over time.

Anxiety disorders are usually treated with **therapy** and medicine. Some people recover completely over time. Others may need ongoing help.

KEY WORD

Therapy: working with a person trained to help with mental health issues.

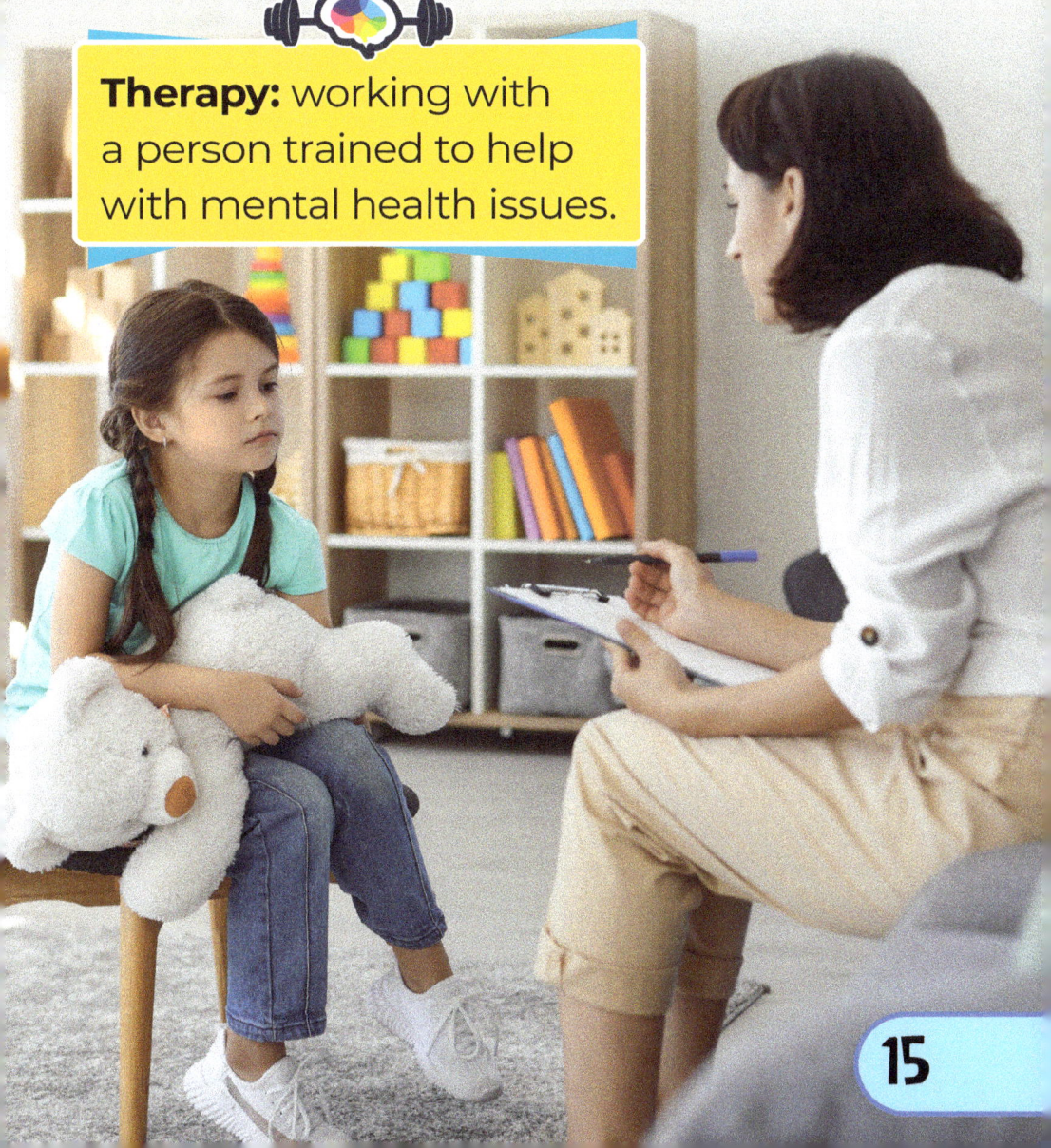

Asking for Help

It is okay to ask for help with anxiety. Other people can help you see stressful things in a new way. Try speaking with an adult you trust. Here are some ways to start the conversation.

"I'm freaking out and I don't know why. Can you talk me through it?"

"I'm really stressed about life. It is making me feel run down. I would like to talk to someone about it. Can you help with that?"

"I'm always worrying about school. I'm afraid of going to class. Can you help me deal with it?"

How to Help Others With Anxiety

If you have a friend or family member with anxiety, there are a few ways you can help.

Talk with them

Ask them what makes them anxious. Remind your friends that feeling anxious sometimes is normal. If needed, encourage them to talk with a parent, teacher, doctor, or school **counselor**.

KEY WORD

Counselor: a person who gives advice to others.

Use distractions

Distract them by pointing out nearby people or things. Helping them focus on the present can reduce their anxiety.

Study anxiety disorders

Read more about anxiety disorders. Share what you know about this mental illness with the ones who are going through it.

the History of Anxiety

Anxiety has had many names throughout history. In 1771, a French doctor named Boissier de Sauvages used the word "panophobias" to describe some anxiety disorders. The word "panophobia" means a fear of everything.

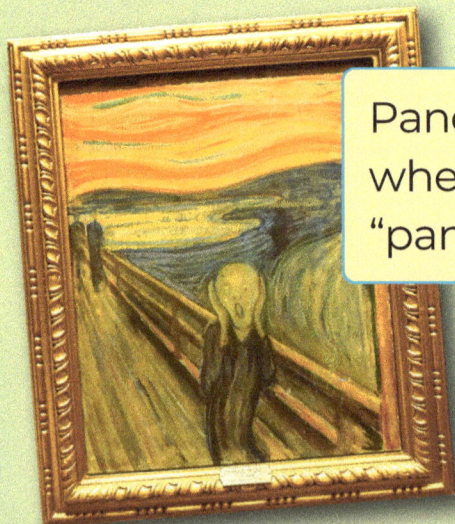

Panophobia is where the word "panic" comes from.

When the American Civil War ended in 1865, many soldiers suffered from panic attacks and shortness of breath. At the time, it was called shell shock by some people. Now it is named **PTSD** or Post Traumatic Stress Disorder.

KEY WORD

PTSD: an anxiety disorder that can happen after a shocking, scary, or dangerous event.

Anxiety Superheroes

There used to be lots of stigma around having anxiety. Today many people speak openly about their anxiety. Talking about anxiety makes it easier to cope with.

Selena Gomez is a popular actress and singer. She has struggled with anxiety, depression, and panic attacks. She helped start WonderMind. This group helps take the stigma out of mental health issues.

Elliot Page is an award-winning actor. Page has battled with extreme anxiety around his **gender identity**. He is open about his struggles with mental health.

KEY WORD

Gender identity: a person's inner sense of whether they are male, female, or something else.

Chris Evans is the actor who played Captain America. He has dealt with lots of anxiety in his life. By speaking out, Evans is making it okay for men to talk about mental health issues.

Anxiety tip 1: Mindfulness

Mindfulness is being aware of the present moment and accepting it as it is. It helps you focus your mind and reduce your anxiety. **Meditation** is a common practice to help you improve your mindfulness.

KEY WORD

Meditation: an exercise of the mind to train attention and awareness.

Deep breathing is another great way to practice mindfulness. To try it, breathe in deeply for four seconds. Hold for four seconds. Then breathe out.

Anxiety Tip 2: Noticing Triggers

When you notice your anxiety, write down what you think at that moment. It may help you to find your **trigger**. That way, you can find ways to stop them from happening.

KEY WORD

Trigger: a thing that makes you feel anxious.

Here are some common triggers:

1. Speaking in front of class

2. Tests and exams

3. Crowds at school

4. Noises and smells

5. Social events

6. Dental appointments

Anxiety tip 3: Spotting False thoughts

People with anxiety often struggle with false thoughts. That means they think and believe bad things about themselves and others. False thoughts make it hard to know what is real.

When you are anxious, ask yourself if what you are thinking is true. Replace bad thoughts with good ones. You can also use a diary to track your thoughts.

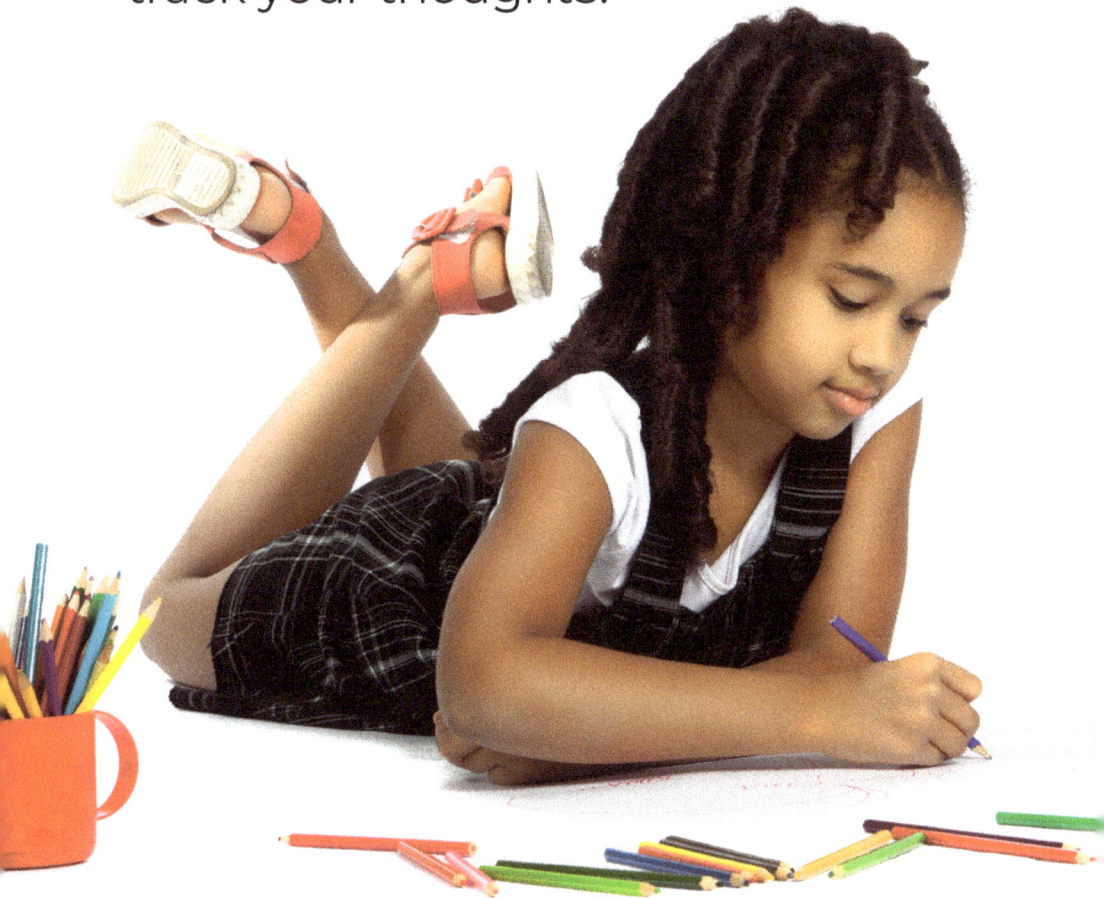

Quiz

Test your knowledge of anxiety by answering the following questions. The questions are based on what you have read in this book. The answers are listed on the bottom of the next page.

1 What is an anxiety disorder?

2 What three parts of your brain are affected by anxiety?

3 What are stress responses meant to do?

4 What is depression?

5 What is therapy?

6 What is a common practice to help you improve your mindfulness?

Explore Other Level 3 Readers.

ENGAGING READERS — LEVEL 3
ADHD
AJ Knight

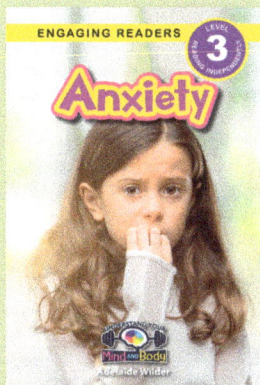

ENGAGING READERS — LEVEL 3
Anxiety
Adelaide Wilder

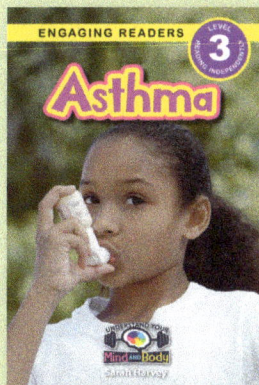

ENGAGING READERS — LEVEL 3
Asthma
Sarah Harvey

ENGAGING READERS — LEVEL 3
Body Image
Adelaide Wilder

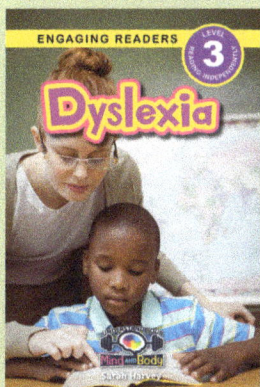

ENGAGING READERS — LEVEL 3
Dyslexia
Sarah Harvey

ENGAGING READERS — LEVEL 3
Diabetes
Kit Caudron-Robinson

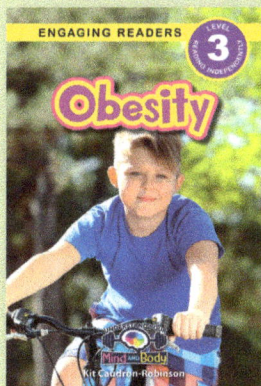

ENGAGING READERS — LEVEL 3
Obesity
Kit Caudron-Robinson

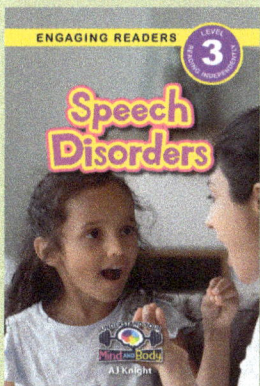

ENGAGING READERS — LEVEL 3
Speech Disorders
AJ Knight

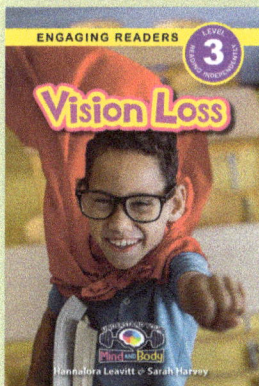

ENGAGING READERS — LEVEL 3
Vision Loss
Hannalora Leavitt & Sarah Harvey

Visit www.engagebooks.com/readers

Answers: 1. A mental illness where you feel extreme or constant worry 2. The brain stem, limbic system, and frontal lobe 3. Keep people safe in dangerous situations 4. A mental illness that causes strong feelings of sadness and lack of hope 5. Working with a person trained to help with mental health issues 6. Deep breathing

www.ingramcontent.com/pod-product-compliance
Lightning Source LLC
Chambersburg PA
CBHW040226040426
42331CB00039B/3368